HELLO BLACK BEAR!

Stephen G. Biddulph

ABOUT HELLO BLACK BEAR!

"Hello Black Bear!" was written because of my boyhood association with bears while living in Yellowstone National Park where my father was a ranger naturalist. I spent every summer living in a little brown cottage on the shores of Yellowstone Lake. I helped my father with his ranger duties and I came to love the flowers, animals, and birds found in the Park. I loved to hike with my father in the mountains where we often came into contact with grizzly and black bears.

In those days, black bears were commonly seen begging for handouts along Yellowstone's highways. People loved to see the bears, some with adorable little cubs, posing for pictures and partaking of cookies and other food that tourists could not resist sharing with them. Sometimes, people forgot that the bears in Yellowstone were wild animals and that they could be unpredictable and dangerous. Some people were bitten and hurt by bears. Feeding Park bears is no longer allowed.

"Hello Black Bear!" is an illustrated limerick written for children to help them learn about bears in an imaginative yet factual way. It teaches children to both appreciate and respect wild animals that share our beautiful world. All living things make our planet a wonderful place and we should learn to love, respect, and protect them so that this world in which we live can remain beautiful.

I hope that you enjoy "Hello Black Bear!"   - Stephen G. Biddulph

Hello Black Bear!
You cuddly, furry
piece of fluff;
I'd like to run my fingers
Through your stuff,
But I don't dare --
Black Bear!

You're pudgy-round
And cuddly-cute;
I'd like to stroke
Your wrinkled snoot,
But I don't dare --
Black Bear!

I'd whisper
In your tufted ear
And tell you that
I have no fear,
But I don't dare --
Black Bear!

I'd pat you on
Your rounded back,
And tickle you on
Your sides of fat,
But I don't dare --
Black Bear!

I'd ride upon
Your bristled hump,
And squeeze the tail
Upon your rump,
But I don't dare --
Black Bear!

You'd chase me up
A tree or two,
And then I'd do
The same to you,
But I don't dare --
Black Bear!

I'd roll with you
In grassy vales;
We'd hike as pals
On mountain trails,
But I don't dare --
Black Bear!

So all this fun
That we might find
Will have to wait
For another time --
Black Bear!

When enmity and fear
Have ceased,
And you and I
Can romp in peace;
'Til then, so long --
Black Bear!

LEARN ABOUT THE BLACK BEAR

The American Black Bear (*Ursus Americanus*) is the smallest and most common of the bears in America. A mature male bear can weigh several hundred pounds and comes in a variety of colors, including cinnamon, blonde, honey, bluish-gray, and, of course, black. Although it may look somewhat slow and awkward, the black bear is quite agile and can easily outrun a human. Their curved, sharp claws are well adapted for climbing trees, unlike its larger distant relative, the grizzly bear. Its adaptable qualities enable the black bear to live in a variety of habitats ranging from high mountain forests to more arid desert areas. The black bear is *omnivorous* in its diet, meaning that it eats a variety of different foods, including twigs, leaves, grass, roots, plants, berries, grubs, insects, beetles, ants, bee larvae, small mammals, and fish.

The black bear mates during the early summer months and frequently gives birth to two cubs, but sometimes as many as four at a time. Cubs are born about mid-winter while the mother is in hibernation, and cubs remain with their mother through the winter and for about another year until they can be on their own. Sows typically produce off-spring every other year. Summer and fall months are spent foraging for food and building up layers of fat to sustain the bear during the winter months when they hibernate and live off their stored fat. They can appear by nature to be cute, good-natured, and even cuddly, but they are wild animals and can be dangerous and unpredictable if approached or provoked. Learn to appreciate and respect this wonderful creation.

MORE ANIMALS TO KNOW

Gold Finch

Chipmunk

Grizzly Bear

Cutthroat Trout

Mountain Lion (Puma)

Cedar Waxwing

Pine (Red) Squirrel

Elk (Wapiti)

American Bison (Buffalo)

Bull Moose

Bighorn Ram

Great Horned Owl